THE PIANO MAKERS

THE PIANO MAKERS

written and photographed by David Anderson

PANTHEON BOOKS

New York

To Kenneth, Jean, and John,
three pianists.

Each manufacturer builds pianos in different ways,
using different methods and tools. The photographs
in this book were taken at the Steinway factory in
New York City. Some of the steps in
their manufacturing process are not used by other
piano makers. The author is indebted to the
employees and management of Steinway & Sons for
their cooperation.

The photograph on page 6 was taken at
Merkin Concert Hall, New York City.

Copyright © 1982 by David Anderson
All rights reserved under International and
Pan-American Copyright Conventions. Published
in the United States by Pantheon Books, a division
of Random House, Inc., New York, and simulta-
neously in Canada by Random House of
Canada Limited, Toronto.
Manufactured in the United States of America
First Edition
Designed by Suzanne Haldane

Library of Congress Cataloging in Publication Data

Anderson, David, 1943–   The piano makers.
Summary: Text and photographs describe the
methods and tools used in making a concert grand
piano at the Steinway factory in New York City.
1. Piano—Construction—Juvenile literature.
[1. Piano—Construction] I. Title.
ML3930.A2A53   786.2'3   82-6513
ISBN 0-394-85353-9   AACR2
ISBN 0-394-95353-3 (lib. bdg.)

THE PIANO MAKERS

PIANOS are made in many sizes and shapes. The largest piano is called the concert grand. Concert grands are used by some of the most demanding players, concert pianists, because they have the fullest range of tone and sound volume. They can be seen and heard in concert halls, in recording studios, and on television. Very few are in homes because they are so big, heavy, and expensive. A concert grand piano is almost nine feet long, weighs one thousand pounds, and has twelve thousand parts.

Because concert grand pianos are played by a relatively small number of people, fewer are made than any other size. During each day very few concert grand pianos are worked on in the factory. However, hundreds of smaller grand pianos, which are the same basic shape as a concert grand, are being built all the time. It takes nearly one year, and four hundred workers and craftspeople, to make a piano.

The part of the piano we see is actually a very well made wooden cabinet. The whole piano, not just the keys and strings, works as a unit to make a good musical sound. That is why it is important to make the piano from the right materials, in the proper shape, so that the notes being played sound strong and alive.

Many different types of wood are used in each piano, including maple, spruce, and pine. Most of the wood comes from the United States, particularly Alaska, and Canada. After it has aged in the lumberyard for one year, the yard foreman inspects each piece to see that it is of good quality, has no defects, and is the proper size.

Then the yard workers load the wood into a drying kiln, a sort of oven as big as a house. It is baked at a low temperature, 160° F., for between three days and three months, depending on what type of wood it is. The heat removes moisture from the wood so that it can be glued easily and will not warp.

9

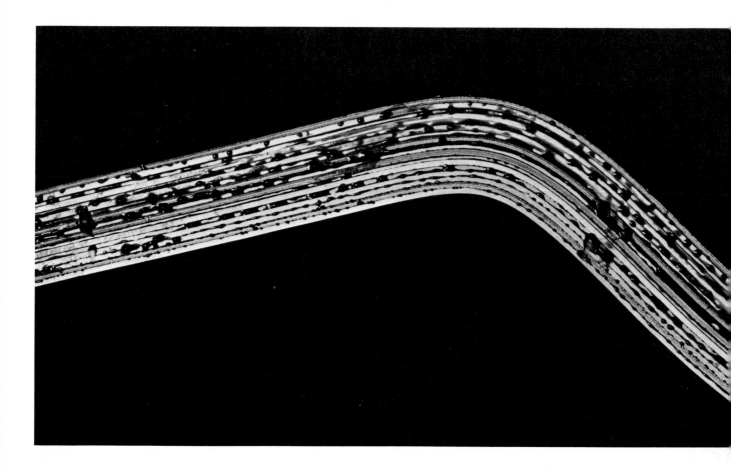

Since it will hold most of the piano's parts, the wooden rim, or case, of the piano is made first.

To make the curved shape of the piano, the wood must be bent. A single thick piece of wood can't be bent; it would break. So instead, sheets of wood about one-eighth of an inch thick called veneers, which have been sliced off big long pieces of wood, are glued together. This process is called lamination. The veneers are very easy to bend, and the laminated wood is stronger and more flexible than a single piece of wood.

Many maple veneers are glued one on top of the other to form a slab of wood three and one-quarter inches thick. The last veneer to be glued on is an extra-thin slice of mahogany, which has the best grain quality and will look best on the outside of the case.

The mahogany veneer is so thin and fragile that the glue must be brushed on by hand rather than applied by machine.

The laminated piece that will become the rim is twenty-one feet long, and so heavy that four men are needed to carry it. 13

The moment the last veneer is in place, they rush it to the rim press, to be
14   bent into shape.

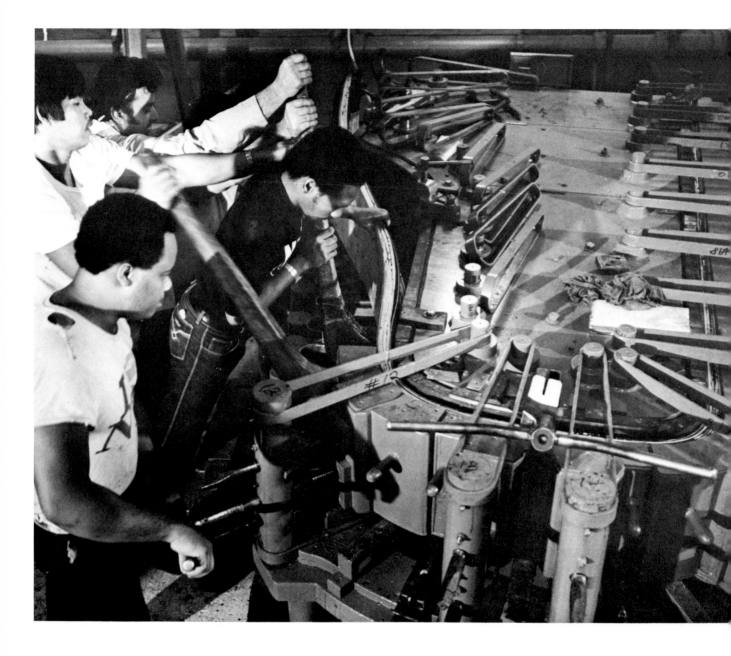

The rim press is a metal frame shaped like a concert grand piano. The workmen tighten vises and clamps to force the wood to bend around it. They work very fast, in complete silence, because the bending must be completed before the special glue dries—and it will dry in only twelve to fifteen minutes!

The wood is left on the press overnight. The next morning the curved rim is taken off the press. It is set aside for about ten weeks to cure—allowing the wood to settle into its new shape.

While shaping the rim requires teamwork, most of the other steps in piano making are done by people who work alone on different parts and sections of the instrument.

Once the rim has cured, the inside surface is shaped and scooped out by a machinist. Chips of wood fly into the air as the router cuts into the rim, making room for the wooden braces that will fit inside.

Other workers install these braces, which strengthen the rim and support the parts of the piano that will go into the case.

When a special case is ordered, a highly skilled carver cuts fancy designs into the wood. Custom carving is generally done on smaller grand pianos, not concert grands. An exception is the concert grand piano in the White House, which has eagles carved on its legs.

    While the rim is being made, other parts of the piano are being built in different areas of the factory.

    After the wood for the piano top, or lid, has been roughly shaped, a wooden template or guide is attached to it. Workmen pull it past a saw that cuts along the edges of the template, giving the top its final shape. They wear face masks so they won't breathe in any sawdust. They also wear metal aprons to protect themselves from being cut by the saw.

The parts of the piano case—rim, top, keyboard cover, and legs—are brought together for finishing.

Cabinetmakers sand the parts smooth.

24   Then a cabinet finisher applies four to six coats of lacquer.

While all this is going on, the soundboard is being constructed.

When a piano key is hit by the pianist's finger, it moves a hammer, which in turn strikes metal strings. The strings vibrate, producing a sound. The sound is amplified by the soundboard in the same way that the beat of a drumstick is amplified by the tight skin of the drum. Since the soundboard is such an important part of the piano, it is made with special skill and care.

Spruce wood is used because its grain is very close together and straight. These qualities help make the soundboard resilient and flexible. A workman carefully selects the different pieces of wood for each soundboard, making sure they are as similar as possible. This ensures that the soundboard will be of excellent quality and will vibrate uniformly.

The pieces of spruce are glued together side by side to form one flat piece of wood. The glued pieces are clamped in a machine called a glue wheel or a windmill press, which can hold eight soundboards at the same time.

After the soundboard is glued, workmen move it through a machine that shapes and sands it. The finished soundboard is eight millimeters thick in the center and five millimeters thick at the edges. A soundboard that has this shape vibrates as one unit, amplifying the sound most efficiently. Only Steinway soundboards are shaped this way.

Using another special press, a worker glues seventeen ribs made of sugar
pine to the bottom of the soundboard. The ribs keep the soundboard slightly
curved upward at the edges, which also helps to amplify the sound.

28

The bridge, which is made of hard rock maple, is glued to the top of the soundboard in yet another special press. The strings of the piano will be stretched across it, and the vibrations of the strings will travel through the bridge to the soundboard.

Whether the bridge consists of one long piece of wood or two separate pieces for treble and bass, its curved shape and its position on the soundboard determine how long a portion of each string can vibrate freely—the "speaking length" of the string. The length of the string, along with its thickness and how tightly it is stretched, determines how high or low the note will be.

The soundboard is temporarily placed in the piano case after the bridge has been glued to it, so that the fit can be very carefully checked.

A worker called the bellyman notches the top of the bridge with a chisel, leaving only a small portion of the top edge higher than the rest. The strings will be stretched across this narrow area, which is covered with black graphite to reduce friction between the strings and the bridge.

At this point the soundboard is complete, but before it is installed it is checked for quality. A supervisor can pound it with his fist and know from the sound it makes whether it will work properly in the piano! If the soundboard passes inspection, it is finally installed in the case.

The plate is the part of the piano that supports the 240 metal strings. It is made of cast iron because it must be very strong. The strings are stretched so tightly that together they exert about 35,000 pounds of tension per square inch. That is equal to the weight of about sixteen cars! Even with the large round holes that are cut in it to reduce its weight, the plate weighs 325 pounds.

The plate is cast at a foundry, not at the piano factory. When it arrives at the factory it is dark gray, and it is rough in places. The rough parts must be ground smooth. The worker who grinds the plate wears ear protectors because of the loud noise made by the grinding wheels hitting the rough surface. He also wears safety glasses to shield his eyes from flying bits of metal.

The strings will be stretched between hooked steel fasteners called hitchpins, attached to the back end of the plate, and steel tuning pins. The tuning pins will be anchored in the pinblock, a heavy block of wood behind the keyboard. So that the 240 tuning pins can come up through the plate from the pinblock underneath, 240 small holes must be drilled into the plate. Holes are also drilled for the bolts that will attach the plate to the rim.

The plate is spray lacquered a bronze color.

After the lacquer has dried, the plate is lowered by a pulley into the piano case, where it is bolted in place. Although it is positioned over the soundboard, the plate does not touch it.

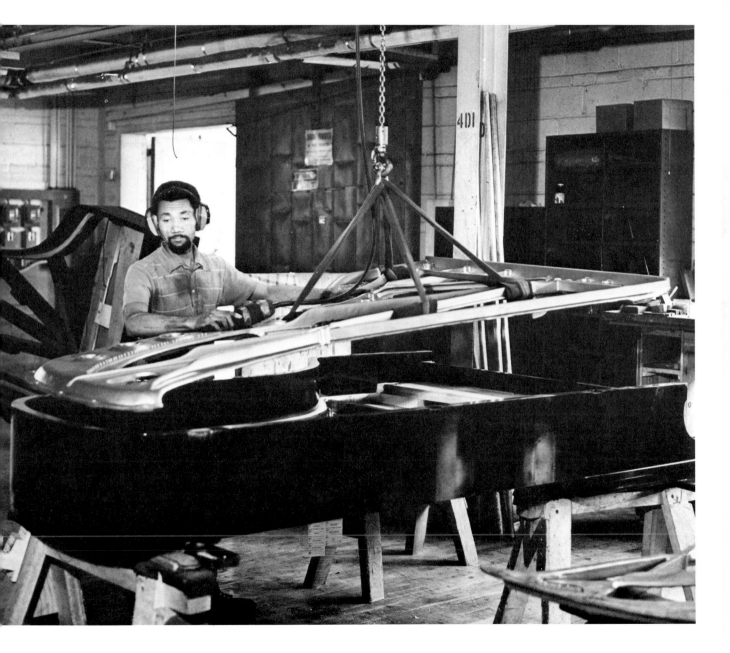

Most of the strings of the piano, like the plate, are not made at the piano factory. But when an extra string is needed, a stringmaker will custom make it at the factory.

The thin, silver-colored steel strings vibrate rapidly and make the treble (higher) notes. The thicker copper-covered strings vibrate more slowly and make the bass (lower) notes. To make a bass string, the stringmaker places thin steel piano wire on a lathe and wraps, or "spins," copper piano wire around it.

Each tuning pin has a rounded end, with a hole for the string to pass through, and a pointed end. The piano stringer hammers the pointed ends of the tuning pins through the holes in the plate, into holes in the pin block. He has to pound the pins very hard, forcing them deep into the pin block so they will fit tightly. It is a very noisy job.

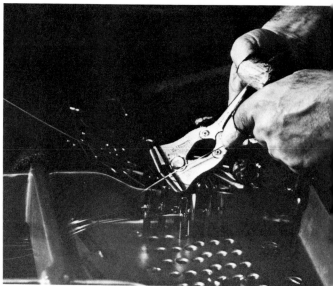

Wearing tape around his fingers to protect them from being cut by the piano wire, the stringer puts on the 201 silver-colored treble strings first— three for each treble note.

For most of these strings, he threads one end of the piece of wire through the hole in a tuning pin and coils the wire neatly around it. Then he stretches the wire across the plate, around a hitchpin, and back to the next tuning pin. He threads it through the pin, coils it around, and cuts it to length with wire cutters. One piece of wire thus makes two treble strings.

Then the stringer puts on the 39 thick copper-covered bass strings, one or two for each bass note. One end of each string is attached to a hitchpin, and the other is threaded through the hole in a tuning pin and coiled around the pin.

39

The bass strings are placed above the treble strings so that they can cross the center of the soundboard, where sound is amplified most effectively. If the strings didn't overlap, the sound-board would have to be much larger.

While the case is being built and strung, other workers are making the action—the parts of the piano that move.

The sound of the piano is produced when hammers strike the strings. The hammers are covered with soft white felt, which is first squeezed into a V shape by a machine. The bass hammers have a thicker layer of felt than the treble hammers; they must be larger in order to make the heavier bass strings vibrate.

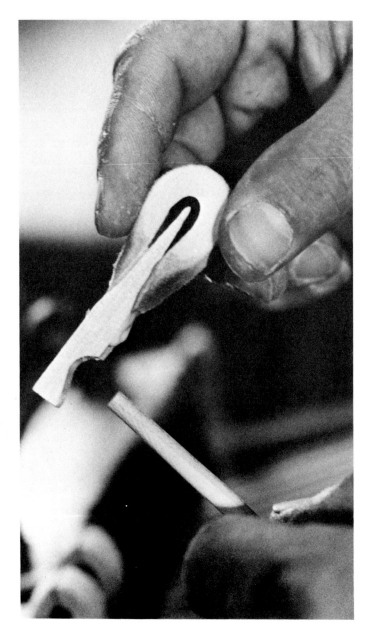

The core of the hammer is a piece of wood called the hammer molding. A layer of firm, dark-colored felt is glued around this to form the inner cushion, and the shaped white felt is glued around that. Each hammer is glued to a hammer shank, a piece of wood five inches long—the "handle" of the hammer. All eighty-eight hammers, one for each key, are mounted on the action frame, which will be installed in the piano case behind the keyboard.

The keys, which are made elsewhere, are constructed of sugar pine covered with plastic. At one time, white key covers were made of ivory. But it is now illegal to kill elephants for their ivory. Unlike the old ivory keys, white plastic keys do not turn yellow with age.

When the keys arrive at the factory they are placed on a key frame one by one to make the keyboard.

The action of the keys is tested to make sure the keys will respond evenly to the pianist's finger pressure. In this "weigh-off" process, a lead weight is placed on each key. A worker observes how far and how fast the key moves when the weight is applied, and makes any necessary adjustments until all eighty-eight keys respond exactly the same way.

Then the action and the keyboard are put into the case.

The damper man installs the dampers, blocks with felt pads that rest on the strings and "damp" the sound. When a key is pressed down, a metal rod lifts the damper off the strings for that note, allowing them to vibrate. When the key is released, the damper automatically returns to the strings to stop them from vibrating. The highest notes on the piano have no dampers, because their short strings don't vibrate for long enough to make dampers necessary.

When the piano's right pedal is pressed, all the dampers are raised, so all the strings can vibrate. All the notes that are played continue to sound until the pedal is released and the dampers return to the strings. The middle pedal lifts only the dampers for those notes being played at the time the pedal is pushed. When the left pedal is pushed down, all the hammers move slightly to one side so that they strike fewer strings, making a softer sound.

The damper man carefully adjusts all the dampers until they rest on the strings with the same amount of pressure and move up and down with the same speed.

The tone regulator is a specialist who makes the delicate adjustments that affect the overall quality of the piano's sound. Using a piece of wood covered with sandpaper, he carefully files each of the newly installed hammers into an egg shape.

The shape of the hammers determines how they will strike the strings and, of course, how the notes will sound. He adjusts each hammer so that it will be lined up to hit the proper strings at dead center.

He sticks the outer felt with needles to make the hammers more resilient, which also changes the sound. It's like hitting a drum with a soft padded stick instead of a hard stick.

The tone regulator has to know just how much shaping and sticking is needed for each and every hammer in order to make the piano sound right. The treble notes should be clear, the bass notes should be full and rich, and the overall sound should blend together. The tone regulator spends about twenty-five hours working on each piano.

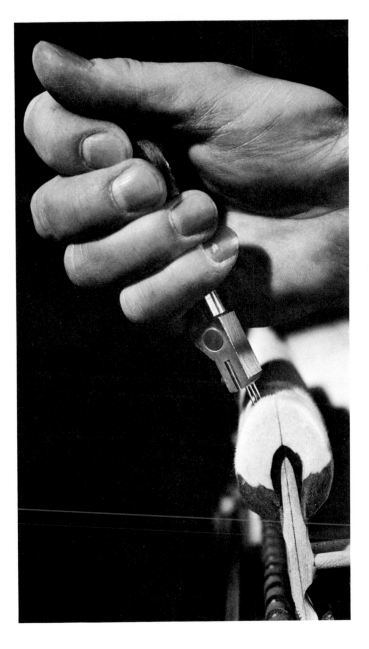

The piano tuner works in a quiet room just large enough for himself and one piano. The piano has already been "chipped," or very roughly tuned, before it is moved into that room.

He begins by tuning the A above middle C. This note will be perfectly in tune when each of its three strings vibrates at the rate of 440 vibrations per second. To check the pitch, the tuner uses an A tuning fork, a specially shaped piece of metal that vibrates exactly 440 times per second when it is struck. He listens to the tuning fork, then plays the A on the piano and listens carefully to the sound. Then he uses a special tool to turn the tuning pin. If the note is too low, that means the string is vibrating too slowly, so he tightens it; if the note is too high, he loosens the string. He plays the note again and again, each time adjusting the tuning pin very slightly, until it sounds right.

He tunes the other strings for that note the same way. Then the other notes are tuned, one string at a time, by comparing them to the A and to one another, until all eighty-eight notes are in tune.

The piano is given a final oil polishing. 51

The legs of the piano are taken off so the case can be put into a narrow
52   wood box. Then it is crated up and shipped out of the factory.

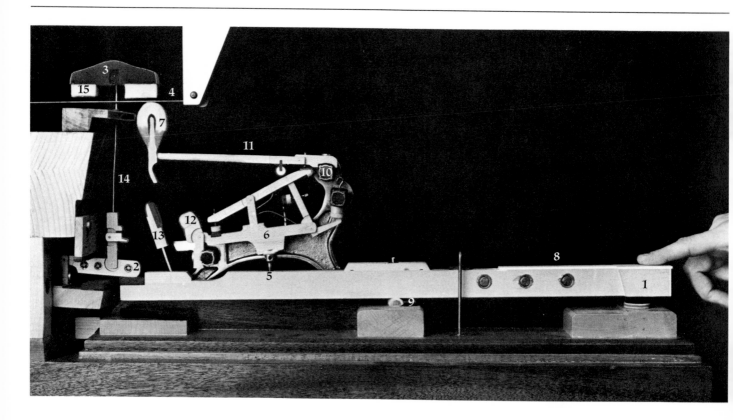

HOW THE PIANO ACTION WORKS

This cutaway view of the piano action shows one key and its movement. When the front of the key (1) is pressed down, the back comes up. It raises the underlever (2) which lifts the damper (3) off the string (4). At the same time, the capstan screw (5) pushes the support (6) up, which in turn flips the hammer (7) so it strikes the string.

When the key is released, the damper returns to its position on the string.

1 key	6 support	11 hammer shank
2 underlever	7 hammer	12 hammer rest
3 damper	8 key cover	13 back check
4 string	9 balance rail bearing	14 damper wire
5 capstan screw	10 hammer rail	15 damper felts

David Anderson was born in Lincoln, Nebraska. He has worked as a motion picture cameraman and has shot TV commercials and sales films. His still photographs are sold through galleries and are represented in the collections of the Brooklyn Museum, the Museum of the City of New York, and the Canadian Center for Architecture in Montreal. THE PIANO MAKERS is the first book for young readers that Mr. Anderson has both written and illustrated. He lives in New York City.

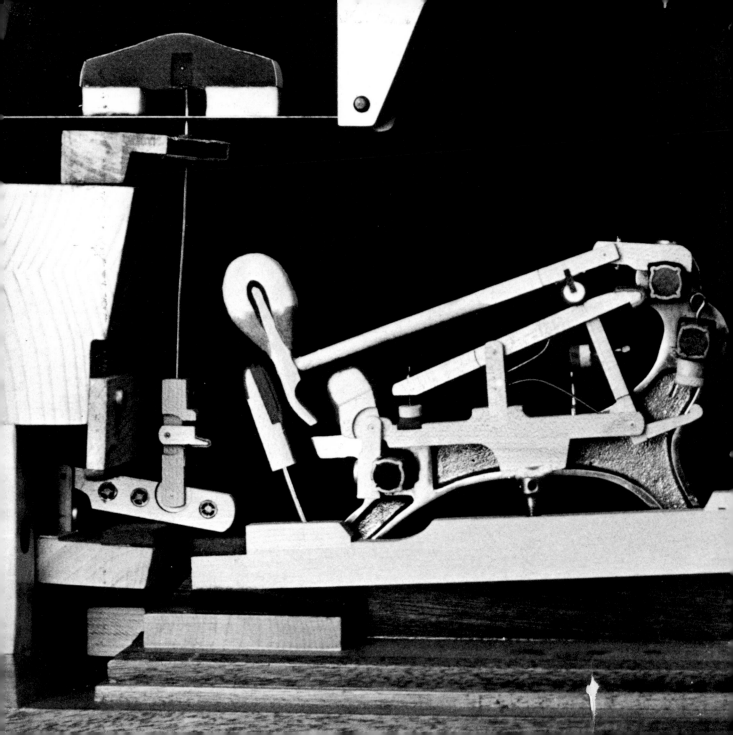